Presentation Skills for Teachers

JEAN M HARRIS

To Chris

Best Wishes

Love Jean

KOGAN
PAGE

London • Philadelphia

Professional Skills for Teachers series

Team-building with Teachers, Judith Chivers
Presentation Skills for Teachers, Jean M Harris
Delegation Skills for Teachers, Jim Knight
Time Management for Teachers, Ian Nelson

This practical series is aimed specifically at developing teachers' management skills. The books include activities and suggestions for things to do, to encourage the reader to think about their own needs and experiences. It will be helpful to have pen and paper handy to write down notes or ideas as you read.

First published in 1995

Kogan Page Limited
120 Pentonville Road
London N1 9JN

British Library Cataloguing in Publication Data

A CIP record for this book is available from the British Library.

ISBN 0 7494 1765 X

Typeset by Saxon Graphics Ltd, Derby
Printed and bound in Great Britain by Biddles Ltd, Guildford and King's Lynn

Contents

CHAPTER 1

Know your Audience and Prepare Objectives

Objectives

When you have completed this chapter you will be able to:

- ask appropriate questions when you are asked to give a presentation
- prepare objectives for your presentation
- research the presentation.

What is a presentation?

During the course of this book we will consider presentations in a variety of situations and for many different purposes. Although presentations may differ widely, there are certain common characteristics. These are:

- It involves a presenter or small group of presenters and an audience.
- The presenter wants to convey information, ideas or arguments.
- The audience wants or needs to understand the information, ideas or arguments.
- The event is logically structured, planned and rehearsed.

- The communication is principally verbal but with support from other media.
- The main communication flow is from presenter to audience.
- Feedback and discussion may be used to clarify and reinforce but not normally to introduce new ideas.

There are other means of giving or sharing information and skills, but these are not termed 'presentations' so we will not be covering these in any depth in this book. However, the skills learned here will be transferable to a wide variety of situations and can be adapted for many.

When first approached

Anyone who has spent time in the education sector is likely to have spoken to groups of pupils for many years. So it is assumed that you can just 'stand up and talk' to anyone. But there are many different types of situation where you may have to give presentations – and they require different skills.

ACTIVITY

Add to the list below *any* situations in your profession where a presentation to a group may be required, and next to each one add a note about the audience.

Situation	Audience
1. Parents' evening	200–300 parents of pupils in one given year.
2. Prize giving	Pupils, parents, governors, visiting dignitaries.

ACTIVITY

Now think about presentations you have given or may be asked to give.

When you are asked to give a presentation or make a speech in public, what is your reaction?

Some possible reactions would be:

'I can't stand up and talk in front of all those people!'
'I'm far too busy to waste time on that sort of thing!'
'I wonder why they chose me?'
'Oh well, I suppose I'll have to do it – yet again. I enjoy it really!'
'Well, I can't have done it too badly last time.'

Whatever your reaction is to the initial request – you need to do it well.

ACTIVITY

Think about presentations that you have attended. What did you like? What did you dislike? Why?

Likes   **Reasons**

Dislikes   **Reasons**

Now review your likes and tick those you want to bring to the presentations *you* will make.

Why is it that some presentations are good and some poor? Often it seems to relate to the personality of the speaker, but good skills can be learned, and poor technique can be avoided. Some of the most common causes of poor presentations are:

- The speaker has not got clear objectives.
- The speaker has not prepared well.
- The level is wrong for the audience.
- The speaker tries to cover too much material.
- There is not enough variety in the presentation.
- There is not enough opportunity for audience participation.
- It is too long.

These are all pitfalls which can be avoided – careful preparation is the key.

ACTIVITY

If you are approached to give a presentation, what questions do you need to ask?

The rest of this chapter will help you to define this list. Each section covers a different aspect of preparation. There is also a separate checklist at the end.

Who is your audience?

This is the most important question to ask. Sometimes the reply will give you most of what you need to know about the audience. 'Graduate recruits to the education authority on their induction course' will tell you that they have a certain academic ability, probably little or no knowledge about the education authority as yet and they are listening to your presentation as part of a course which they are obliged to attend.

The following is an example of a different situation.

Example

> Ian was invited to give a presentation to members of a Chamber of Commerce about the current examination system as it related to employers.
>
> He delivered a general talk about all school exams. The majority of the time was taken up with background information about the syllabus and teaching methods. Six of the 12 people present already had pupils at the school and knew its methods well. Two others were school governors.

Ian's lack of audience research meant that most of his audience did not get what they wanted and wasted time listening to things they already knew.

It is important that you know not only *who* you are talking to, but *why* they are attending, *what* they expect to get out of it and *what* they already know about the subject. You may only be able to guess at some of the answers but it will help you to clarify *why* you are giving the talk and to pitch it at the best level for the audience.

Setting aims and objectives

Having found out all you can about the presentation, who it is for and what they need to know, you are now able to set the aims and objectives.

What aims could a presentation have?

Aims are broader and more general than objectives. The general aims of a presentation will give the structure and purpose to your presentation. When first thinking of your aims you should consider whether your presentation needs to achieve any of the following:

- to inform (for example, the exam results of a school)
- to educate (for example, presenting health and safety measures)
- to persuade (for example, to persuade prospective parents to choose your school)
- to change opinions or attitudes (for example, presenting a new approach to staff development).

Many presentations will have a mixture of these types of aim, and many will also include aims such as to be challenging or to be entertaining. All should include 'to satisfy the need of the audience'.

The aims will give some broad guidance, but more specific objectives will be needed to guide your presentation more precisely.

Objectives

ACTIVITY

What do you understand by an 'objective'? Write down a brief description.

The following notes will explain the purpose of objectives in the context of giving a presentation. Your description above may differ in detail but should fit these notes in general terms.

It is fundamental that you are clear about the reason why the presentation is being given; you need to know its aims and why a presentation is the best way of meeting this particular need. Objectives are the essential tools to ensure that you focus on the aim. They also act as measures to help you judge how successful the presentation has been. We are concerned here with learning objectives: these are intended to be the outcome of your presentation for your audience.

Objectives must be *specific*, *achievable* and if possible *measurable*. They should describe clearly what the audience will know or be able to do at the end of the presentation. Even if you cannot measure the outcomes yourself, they will give a focus for planning the materials in your presentation. Just like objectives for any lesson you teach, the objectives for your presentation must be *learner-* or *audience-centred* – you must plan with the needs of the audience in mind at all times. A definition of an objective is: *'something sought or aimed at'.*

An example of an objective which is too general and is *speaker-* not *audience*-centred is:

To introduce the revised National Curriculum for 5- to 11-year-olds to a parents' meeting.

Better objectives would be:

– to explain the purpose of the revisions to the National Curriculum for 5- to 11-year-olds;
– to list the changes in programmes of study and attainment targets;
– to explain the effects of the changes on teaching and learning in the classroom.

These are *learner-* or *audience*-centred objectives which will help the speaker decide what to emphasize.

Each chapter in this book begins with a set of objectives; they are examples of how objectives can be phrased. You may have your own approach built on experience in lesson planning, but before you begin you must be perfectly clear why you are making the presentation. This should include whether the intention is to persuade, inform, stimulate, challenge or promote. Take time to define the objectives carefully; this will help you to design the content of the presentation to achieve the aims.

You may have been given some objectives by whoever asked you to give the presentation, but you will still need to set your own, in your own words and for your own guidance.

ACTIVITY

Think about a talk or presentation you may have given in the past. Did you have objectives? If so – what were they? Write them here:

If you did not have objectives, are you *really* sure what the purpose of the presentation was?

Yes   No

If you did not have objectives, or think they could have been improved, write down the new objectives here:

Are they *clear*? If not, read the section on objectives again to see what more you need to know about your audience and the purpose of the presentation. The checklist at the end of this chapter will help.

How do aims and objectives help?

Setting aims will enable you to define what you want to achieve through your presentation. They will help you to decide what should and should not be included and will help you to keep your presentation plan on track.

They will have a bearing on the structure, content, angle, style and level.

It is likely that your audience will include individuals of varying knowledge and ability. It may be that you cannot satisfy the personal needs of everyone across a wide spectrum. Therefore it is important that you state the objectives of your presentation clearly at the beginning. The audience will then know what you are trying to achieve with this presentation.

Researching the subject

Having found out what you are expected to talk about, the basic knowledge level of your audience and how much detail you need, you must now gather together all the information.

This may include your own material, gathering information from colleagues, background reading and other activities. You may be very familiar with the topic and feel that you do not need to carry out any research. But before you discard the idea of research, go back to your objectives and what you know about the audience, and make sure you do have all the information you need. Ask yourself:

Could it be reinforced by some facts and figures?
Do I need to update my knowledge?
Could it be enhanced by a few examples or case studies which colleagues might have?

You may later discard some of the detail, but before you begin planning you must have in mind the broad picture of the topic. It is always useful to find out a little more than you need for the presentation, to help you to answer questions which may be put by the audience.

At this stage you can also collect back-up materials which may be useful for preparing visual aids.

The following checklist covers the three key areas already described but includes a number of other important questions you must ask to help with your planning.

Checklist

Questions to ask before you begin detailed preparation
What is the event?
What date and time is it to take place?

What is the subject?

What are the expected/desired outcomes?

What is the theme and purpose of the whole event?

Will there be other speakers and a chairperson? If so – who?

What topics will any other speakers be covering?

Where does my part fit in the programme?

Will I be giving a straight talk or involved in discussion, and will there be questions?

How long have I got?

Where will it take place?

What is the venue like (eg, hall, small room, etc.)?

What facilities does it have, or can be provided (eg, projector, flip chart)?

Who are the audience?

What is their level of knowledge of this subject?

Why are the audience attending; is it by invitation or a public event?

How many people are expected to attend?

Do I have to gain approval of what I propose to say – if so, when and from whom?

You could copy this checklist and turn it into a job aid which you can use later.

Summary

You must find out as much as possible about the audience to enable you to give the right presentation to meet their needs. You will also need some background about the event at which you will speak. Make sure that you have answers to all the questions in the checklist above. This will help you prepare appropriate objectives and plan the presentation to achieve them.

You must set yourself objectives for the presentation. Are your objectives clear, specific and learner/audience-centred? Then gather together all the information about the topic relevant to those objectives before you start to plan the detail.

CHAPTER 2
Preparing the Presentation

Objectives

When you have completed this chapter you will be able to:

- select the most appropriate method of presentation
- identify and plan the key points of your presentation
- structure your presentation
- plan to make the best use of time available
- write your presentation
- know one technique to make notes to suit your presentation style.

Why prepare?

ACTIVITY

If you think preparation *is* important, write down here the single most important reason for preparation.

If you do *not* think preparation is important, write down here why you believe you do not need to prepare.

The rest of this chapter will explain to you why preparation is important, and describe the benefits. As much as 90 per cent of time and effort could be spent in preparation, so for a half hour talk preparation might take 4.5 hours. This is not a hard and fast rule and longer presentations are likely to have a lower percentage of preparation time.

Before a motor company can build a car there need to be designs, prototypes, then plans for the production process. The building of a car is a complex task involving many people and activities, so it is unlikely that anyone would start the process without some objectives and plans.

No one would suggest that giving a lesson is that complex, but in your early days in teaching or lecturing you probably had to produce lesson plans for your tutor or department head. Now you may still do this, but possibly in a less formal way. As we get more experienced, we tend to rely on that experience more and planning less. But that is not always a good thing. Planning something, even a topic with which you are familiar, can help you to make sure you have all the latest facts available, and give you an opportunity to add new materials or take a new approach.

Preparation is always important. Even speakers who are well versed in their subjects need to prepare if they are to give their best and make the most useful presentation to the audience. Preparation will help you to:

- present the information the audience needs to know;
- present in a way that is appropriate for your audience and easy to understand;
- give yourself the confidence that you know what you are doing so that you can present well;
- give a good account of your organization as well as yourself.

You will see that three of the four points above are related to others – the audience and your organization. Preparation is not only to your advantage: it also helps others to get the most benefit from the occasion. The time spent in planning and preparation will pay back great dividends in the end.

Consequences and benefits

The consequences of *not* planning could be:

the presenter is unsure of the material;
the presenter is not believable;
the presentation does not fit its allotted time;
the material is confused and difficult to understand;
the presentation is jumbled and disjointed because it has no logical order;
irrelevant material is included and wastes time;
relevant material is forgotten by the presenter and missed out.

The benefits of planning are:

the presenter is believable;
the presenter is calm, in control and not nervous;
the presentation fits its allotted time;
the flow of the material is logical so it is easy to follow;
all points are covered completely;
only relevant material is included.

Up to this stage you should have:

- researched the subject and collected all the information;
- found out the background to the presentation and the event;
- collected information about the audience;
- set objectives for your contribution.

Before you organize the content you will need to decide what type of presentation you are going to give.

Which method to use

ACTIVITY

Consider the following situations and decide which method from the following list would be most suitable:

presentation
brainstorm with small group
group training session
practical training session
self-study pack

A – Explain the benefits of sending your child to this
  school.
B – Teach a group of staff how to use a new computer
  system.
C – Establish ways of reducing departmental budgets.
D – Provide induction on schools in the Authority to
  new LEA clerical staff.
E – develop improved time management skills among a
  group of school advisers.

The answers may seem obvious, but the important learning
point is the reasons why each method should be chosen:

presentations are most successful where there are
  predetermined facts. The aim is to persuade, inform,
  educate or change opinions; little audience
  participation is essential;

brainstorming with small groups is most successful when
  the opinions and ideas of others are needed; the facts
  are not predetermined; participation and cooperation
  are essential for success;

group training sessions are most successful when ideas
  should be drawn from within the group; participants
  should be given the opportunity to challenge, ask
  questions and discuss the principles involved;

practical training sessions are most successful when
  hands-on training is needed for learning to take place;
  practical assessment is needed to monitor effectiveness;

self-study packs are most useful when new employees are
  started at different times and it would be difficult to
  justify a traditional course; information is peculiar to a
  limited number of users and not obtainable on the open

market; information is complicated or difficult to absorb, so should be taken at the learner's own pace.

You may already have been told which method you are going to use (eg, 'Give a short lecture' or 'Run a discussion group') but if you have a free choice you need to select the most appropriate method.

If you go back to the objectives you can consider the purpose of this event. Is it to:

- give information;
- teach skills;
- change attitudes, persuade or 'sell' an idea;
- a combination of any of these?

Most of the audience will be there because they want to learn something from you; by now you should have a clear idea of what that is. Assuming that some form of presentation is required, there is more than one way of doing this.

The methods

There are three main methods of giving a presentation:

an instructional talk
vocational
discussion.

An *instructional talk* is best for giving information to a number of people, especially large groups. This method is adaptable and could involve a mixture of methods such as: a talk or lecture; visual aids; questions; discussion. The technique is also useful as preparation for practical work later.

The *vocational* method is best for situations where skills are to be taught – this could be using mental skills (calculating budgets), physical skills (operating a computer) or social skills (dealing with people). It can use similar techniques as the instructional talk, but is also likely to involve demonstration or even practical work.

The *discussion* method is useful when you are trying to change attitudes or consider problems rather than to teach facts. It does not work well with very large groups so is frequently used for smaller events or where one large group can be divided into a number of small 'break out' or 'discussion' groups. It also requires the audience to have some knowledge of the subject or enough information to have opinions on it.

A presentation can include some aspects of more than one method and you can select your methods by considering:

the purpose of the event
the needs and experience of the target audience
the size of the audience
the venue and facilities available
the time available
your own skills – can you handle one method better than
   another?

An example of an event which would use the presentation method would be:

Purpose:	To introduce new school governors to the requirements of the new National Curriculum
Audience:	Newly appointed school governors
Number:	20
Venue:	School hall or classroom; OHP and flip chart.
Time:	45 minutes
Content:	1. Structure of the NC and implementation dates
	2. Programmes of study and attainment targets
	3. Implications for classroom delivery.

In this book we will be concentrating on the instructional talk, but much of the advice is also appropriate to aspects of the other techniques.

When you have decided which technique you will use and gathered your information together, the next stage is to organize the content to fulfil the objectives.

Select and organize the content

When you have completed your research you may have quite a lot of information about your topic. But how will you present it to the audience in the most effective way?

First you need to sort the information out into learning points, topics or sub-headings. Then you should go back to your objectives and ask, 'What does this audience really want to know or understand?' Finally, go through your material and for each piece of information ask:

Is this relevant to the objectives?
Is this an essential fact they need to know?
Is this useful but not essential?
Is it a good illustration or further explanation of the topic?

If it is not relevant *cross it out* – and be ruthless!
If it is essential, write '*must*' next to it.
If it is useful additional information, write '*should*' next to it.
If it is a good illustration or further explanation, write '*could*' next to it.

You will now have information organized into a series of learning points or topics and be clear about the importance of each piece of information within those. This is the basis of the information you are going to put across to your audience.

The next step is to sort this into a logical sequence. It must flow smoothly from one point to the next, beginning with the basics or what the audience already knows, moving towards the more complex. Less important or supporting information can be added only if you have time, otherwise it can be covered in a handout.

Making it interesting

Having established the most appropriate method for your presentation and collected all the material to achieve understanding, you need to consider how to make it interesting. Although the descriptions and explanations of the facts may be what is required, you also need to capture and keep the audience's attention. We will talk about other techniques for this later in Chapters 5 and 6, and we will explain the use of other media in Chapter 3, but making the presentation interesting will require some work from you at this preparation stage.

ACTIVITY

Start a story diary. In it write down anecdotes and amusing stories that relate to your job and any topics you may have to talk about.

Just make brief notes or bullet points to bring the story to mind when you need it.

You can use your diary to bring interesting or amusing examples to mind to help make your future presentations more interesting. Presentations benefit from a human dimension – if they are just shovels full of facts and figures they can be very boring.

You will also benefit from considering the words you use. Try to develop a rich and varied vocabulary to paint pictures with words. This can make your presentation interesting and memorable as well as helping to make some points clearer.

Planning the structure

Having decided what method you are going to use and what you intend to present, you can now structure your presentation. Any presentation can be divided up into three sections:

the introduction (usually about 10 per cent of the time)
the main body (usually about 75 per cent)
the conclusion (usually about 15 per cent).

The figures are not hard and fast rules, but a guide which you may find useful.

The introduction

Getting off on the right foot is important for both you and your audience. It will be helpful for the audience if they know at the outset:

- who you are (this should also include why you are giving the presentation – your experience in this area);
- what you are going to talk about, its aim and purpose;
- why the subject matters to them;
- what the structure of the talk will be – including main themes;
- when questions from the audience will be welcomed;
- whether handouts will be available – so they can decide whether or not to take notes;
- whether there will be any visual aids or not;
- how long you will be talking;
- whether you will be available for consultation afterwards.

The introduction should inform the audience of what you are going to do and why, but it must also stimulate their interest. Most audiences will listen out of politeness, but if you can give them powerful reasons for wanting to listen and learn they will be more attentive and supportive. We will come back to this again in Chapter 6.

The main body

The main body of the presentation gives the detail of the subject to the audience. It should help them to understand and remember the information as well as know how to use or apply it.

If the main body of the talk is a long section you may need to help the audience follow it. You can do this in a number of ways:

- refer back to your structure which you will have explained in the introduction, and summarize at appropriate stages;
- invite and ask questions to clarify understanding if the situation permits;
- use visual aids to bring variety and clarification;
- use examples or anecdotes, especially ones which are relevant and meaningful to this particular audience.

The conclusion

The purpose of the conclusion is to:

- give a summary to help the audience to remember the main points of the presentation;
- highlight key messages relevant to the audience;
- where appropriate, also give the audience the opportunity to ask questions to clear up any misunderstandings or develop points.

It should be concise. Use simple terms and be 'punchy'. Try to leave the audience feeling enthusiastic and motivated and believing that this has been a worthwhile experience. If the final session includes questions, make sure you leave time to draw this to a conclusion in the way you want to at the end – we will look again at dealing with questions in Chapter 6.

Writing the brief

Having researched the topic, collected the information and organized it into a structure, you will need to write the material up in a way that you can use in your presentation. There are four main ways of doing this:

1. Write it all out word for word as a script for a speech.
2. Write 'headlines' on a sheet of paper: these will be your topic or paragraph headings.
3. Write key points as memory joggers on cue cards.
4. Write structured notes which you can develop or modify as you talk.

Each of these methods has advantages and disadvantages.

ACTIVITY

Think about a presentation you have attended where the speaker read from a prepared script. As a recipient, did it work well and did you enjoy it? If you found it good – what were the reasons? If not – why didn't you enjoy it? Make a note of the main reasons here.

Think of another presentation where the speaker used a different method. Consider the advantages and disadvantages of this method again and make some notes of your reactions.

When you are giving a presentation, you should think about the needs of the audience, and the activity above puts you in the place of the audience and what they may have preferred. Before we go on to look in more detail at the pros and cons of the different methods, there is another person to take account of – you. Your own preference should also be taken into account. It is no good using a method with which you are uncomfortable: you will not give your best.

A script

Advantages
Essential if the speech has to be word perfect (eg, a legal document).
Can be appropriate for very formal occasions.
Useful for last-minute stand-ins who may not be as familiar with the topic as the original presenter.

Disadvantages

It is totally inflexible.

There is a danger of the speaker sounding stilted, detached and insincere.

We do not speak as we write and writing a script to speak is a rare skill.

It isolates the speaker and loses eye contact with the audience.

Sometimes may require the help of an assistant to use visual aids.

Requires concentration to keep the place in the notes; difficult to find again if the place is lost.

Headlines

Advantages

Allows for flexibility of approach and interaction with the audience.

Helps to remind speaker of main points.

Avoids the temptation to read out aloud.

Allows for a natural delivery.

Ensures all main topics are covered and in the right order.

Keeps the speaker on course.

Disadvantages

Requires very thorough preparation.

Requires complete familiarity with the subject.

May lack some details required.

Cue cards

Advantages

As for headlines plus:

More information to jog memory.

Easily held in the hands, so useful if no table, or speaker wishes to move around.

Unobtrusive for the audience.

Disadvantages

May lack some of the details you need.

Structured notes

Advantages
Most flexible method.
Allows interaction with the audience.
Ensures all main topics are covered in the right order.
Allows natural speech.
Gives more information than headlines or cue cards.

Disadvantages
May have too much information to be easy to follow.

You can use combinations of these systems to suit your needs. If you are writing notes, remember to keep them simple – don't put in too much detail. Make sure you are comfortable with the system, and develop and change it as your needs change. Often presenters find that they move from more to less detail as they gain confidence.

Remember to number your sheets or cards, or tie them together (very loosely so they turn easily). You don't want to drop them and give your presentation in the wrong order!

Must, should and could

When you have written out your notes go through them and decide which parts are essential ('musts') which areas are useful to explain or develop ideas ('shoulds') and which you could leave out as they are non-essential enhancements ('coulds').

Highlight your 'musts' in one colour and the 'shoulds' in another. Then if you are short of time or have to adapt your talk, you can easily see which are the most essential areas and which you could cut down on or omit.

Visual aids

If you are using any visual aids or other media you should also make a note of this in your notes. A simple reference in the margin, for example, 'OHP 1 – Classroom layout', will usually be sufficient to remind you to put the visual up at the right time. (We will look at preparing good visual aids in Chapter 3.)

Timing the presentation

You need to think about timing when you are preparing your presentation. It is not sufficient to note the 'musts, shoulds and coulds'; you also need to plan timing in at this stage.

Example

A freelance trainer, very experienced in giving presentations, was asked to speak at a seminar for career teachers. She was to be the last of three speakers over coffee after lunch. Each was given exactly five minutes to speak about their company.

The rules were that after five minutes the gavel was banged and the speaker had one minute left. After six minutes the gavel was banged again and the speaker had to stop.

Rather unusually for her, the trainer first wrote her talk out word for word. She then trimmed some detail and made cue cards of the key points from this. She practised it twice with a colleague and a stop watch.

The first speaker started well with an amusing anecdote and spoke about how he had been asked to give the talk. He was just getting into his stride when the gavel banged, so he was able to refer to his product only briefly when the gavel banged for the second time and he had to stop.

The second speaker was rather nervous but had copious notes and proceeded to plough through them. When the first gavel banged he was only half way through; he rushed on trying to get to the end of his inflexible script, but when the second gavel banged he was left in mid-air.

The trainer used her notes to keep her on course, made all her key points and was just thanking the audience for their attention when the first gavel banged. The apparently large amount of preparation for a small job paid off – it can be harder to give a short talk than a long one.

No matter how experienced you are, timing and rehearsal are important. Speakers often overrun their time because they did not prepare well. Time overruns are bad manners –

to your audience, to your hosts and to any following speakers. This could be an irritation and detract from what you have to say.

ACTIVITY

In Chapter 1 we discussed setting objectives for a presentation.

If you had to explain 'setting objectives' to a colleague, what are the points you would make? You may wish to write down some notes here.

Now imagine that you only have two minutes to talk about the topic. Select your 'must' points, organize them into a logical order, then speak them out loud *timing yourself carefully.*

How long did you take? Did it take more or less time than you thought? Guessing how long something will take is not easy, so you may have to work at this until you become more experienced.

One way to get the timing right is to add together all the elements or topics in your presentation. For example:

introduction – 5 minutes;
questions – 10 minutes;
conclusion – 7 minutes.

This means that in a total time of 45 minutes, you are left with 23 minutes for the main body. Is this enough time or do you want to reorganize it? Remember you may need to include time for visual aids. If you want to change the timing, you can do it easily at this stage and arrange your notes accordingly.

Once you have divided your talk up this way you can sub-divide the main body into time 'chunks' to allow more time for the more important or complex issues.

The only truly reliable way to time the presentation is to rehearse it – not just in your head but really talk it right through with the visual aids you will use. We will consider rehearsal in more detail in Chapter 4.

Whichever method of making notes you have chosen, it will be useful if you put time check points in the margins. This way you can keep an eye on how you are doing and adjust as appropriate. This is where the system of 'musts, shoulds and coulds' can come in handy to slow down or speed up your presentation without compromising the pace of your speech.

When you have timed your presentation, beware of padding it out too much. If the dummy run takes 20–25 minutes, the actual presentation could take up to five minutes longer. Finishing early is preferable to inserting useless extras as time-fillers.

What if?

Think about what could go wrong with your presentation. This might not seem very encouraging, but if you are prepared, a problem or change of plans is less likely to catch you off guard and it will not turn into a disaster.

ACTIVITY

If you have a presentation to prepare, make a note here of the things which could go wrong. Or if you have had some experiences of things which have gone wrong, list them here.

Now go back to the list and mark with a 'P' those which could be avoided by good planning. Remember these next time you plan a presentation. For the others, try to think of a solution, and note this for future reference. You could ask experienced colleagues what they have done in similar circumstances and add their solutions to your bank of 'fallback' solutions. The following are some examples of problems and how to avoid them:

> You run over time – better planning and rehearsal could avoid this.
> The speaker before you runs over time – have the 'musts, shoulds and coulds' marked on your notes and cut out the 'coulds' and (if necessary) the 'shoulds' as well.
> You have planned to use 35mm slides and there is only an OHP available – try to take your visual aids in both formats.
> You have planned to use slides or the OHP and there is a power cut – try to have the main visual aids as handouts (one set the organizer could photocopy may be sufficient) and make sure you can organize your notes so you can talk without the pictures. If the power cut totally blacks out the room, you may not be able to continue anyway!

By thinking of situations you have seen or experienced and by talking to others, you will be able to extend this list. That should give you the confidence that you can overcome most problems. Remember, if difficulties are due to situations beyond your control, the audience will probably be sympathetic.

Summary

A good presentation begins with good planning. You will need to:

- select your information to fit the objectives;
- choose the most appropriate method for your presentation;

- organize your information into a logical structure within the three areas – introduction, main body and conclusion;
- decide on the 'musts, shoulds and coulds' and note these;
- write out your notes in the way you want to use – script, headlines, cue cards or structured notes;
- time it and adjust accordingly; write time notes in the margin of your notes or cards.

The *introduction* should:

- raise interest in the topic by relating it to the audience's needs;
- explain the aim and purpose of the session;
- describe the order of presentation (use a visual aid to help if possible);
- state whether or not you want to take questions, and if so, when;
- state what, if any, handouts or follow-up papers are available and what they cover

The *main body* of the presentation should:

- give all the relevant facts;
- use examples, visual aids and other techniques to illustrate, add variety and make the information clear.

The *conclusion* should:

- summarize the main points of the presentation;
- allow the audience to clarify if necessary;
- bring the presentation to a satisfying end.

Think about what could go wrong or be changed, and try to plan fall-back positions to overcome likely problems.

CHAPTER 3
Visual Aids

Objectives

When you have completed this chapter you will be able to

- describe when and why to use visual aids
- describe the main uses of four types of visual aid
- state the advantages and disadvantages of these aids
- decide which is most suitable for a given situation
- prepare effective visual aids
- use your visual aids efficiently.

The use and purpose of visual aids

Have you watched a speaker put a slide on upside down then say, 'I seem to have got this the wrong way up!' or, 'I never could get the hang of this new technology'?

If so, it would not be surprising – what is surprising is that so many speakers still make such mistakes. Remarks like this do nothing for the speaker's credibility. Audiences are used to high-technology equipment and have little sympathy for those who get it wrong. It is unprofessional and irritates the audience.

If you are going to use visual aids at all they must be good and you must use them well.

ACTIVITY

List as many reasons as you can think of why you *should* use visual aids in a presentation.

Now list reasons why you might *not* want to use them.

If your reasons for using visual aids are to save you talking or fill the time – that is not good enough. If the reasons for not using them are because you do not know how to, then this chapter will help you.

Good visual aids can lift an otherwise mundane session. Poor visual aids can do little good and much harm. When you are planning a presentation you should always consider whether you want to use visual aids, but the first question is to think carefully *why* you need them and what they will *add* to your presentation.

Main types of visual aids

There are five main visual aids most commonly used:

flip chart
overhead projector
35mm slide projector
video
computers.

Each has its uses and there are situations where some are more useful or appropriate than others. The following sections explain the advantages and disadvantages of each.

Flip chart

Advantages
It is cheap.
The pages are easy to prepare.
It can be used anywhere.
It does not require a power supply.
It can be prepared in advance and easily carried.
It can be used as a notepad during the presentation.

Disadvantages
It is difficult to see from a distance.
The pages get scruffy if used more than once.
Few people have good enough freehand writing to make it look professional.

Overhead projector

Advantages
It is simple to operate.
The speaker can take up a position in front of the audience and still maintain eye contact while using the projector.
The speaker can easily point to details on the foil.
It does not need blackouts (but may be difficult to see in very bright light).
Foils can be prepared in advance.
Foils can be written/drawn on while being displayed (but beware of misusing this technique).
Can be inexpensive to produce in-house.

Disadvantages
Cannot project as large as slides and still be clear.
Needs a power supply.
The speaker may be tempted to look at the screen, rather than the foil, and so turn their back on the audience.
There is a temptation to produce hand-written text.
Photograph foils are very expensive to produce.

35mm slide projector

Advantages
Can be shown to both very large and small groups.
Can show actual photographs as well as graphics.
When good slides are used, adds a professional image to
the presentation.

Disadvantages
Projectors can be expensive.
Needs a power supply.
Professional slides can be expensive.
Requires a blackout, and can lose audience contact for the
speaker.
Needs a remote control or assistant to change slides.

Video

Advantages
Can show moving pictures and sequences of events.
Adds sound to vision.
Can be used to have an emotional impact on the audience.
Can show complex processes which are difficult to describe.
Can show real people doing real activities.
Can provide a good change of pace or style.

Disadvantages
Temptation to use 'home movie' footage can give an
unprofessional image.
Professionally made video (not 'off-the-shelf') is expensive.
Off-the-shelf videos are usually of general, not specific,
interest and must be used sparingly.
The speaker can lose touch with the audience when the
video is playing.
Can only be used for large groups with expensive
specialist projector.

Computers

Advantages
Can show exactly what is on the screen when
demonstrating software.

With appropriate software could show animation.
Visuals can be changed, customized and updated quickly and easily.

Disadvantages
Taking the computer off-site can be difficult, and damage is expensive.
Moving the software from one machine to another may have compatibility problems.
You need plenty of time in the room to set up and test all aspects of the equipment and software to avoid problems.
Without expensive projection equipment computer screens are too small for more than a few to watch.
You may require specialist technical help.
Requires a reliable power source.

Fit your choice to the venue, material and audience

Flip chart

This is best used when you are talking to small groups. It is also useful when you want to involve the audience and make notes, such as during a brainstorming session.

If you are unsure of the availability of a power supply and cannot check the venue before the presentation, the flip chart is a good stand-by.

If you are using one make sure that you write large and clearly enough for all the group to read it. Prepare as much as possible before the presentation and only write when in front of the group if this is essential, as in brainstorming or noting their points to discuss.

Position it where it will not be obscured by the heads of the people in front.

Overhead projector

It is best used for small to medium-sized groups and can usually be used in a room where there is no blackout.

It can be used for pictures, charts or diagrams as well as words. If you cannot have foils produced professionally, you can produce them with many computer DTP (desk-top publishing) packages, or with a photocopier and photo-sensitive foil from good originals. Be careful not to overcrowd your foils or make them too complex (see the next section on producing good visual aids).

35mm projector

Unless you have access to a computer and DTP package or are using your own photographs, you will need to have your slides made professionally. If producing them yourself, again you should look at the guidelines in the next section.

Slides are especially useful for large groups and where you want to show photographs.

Video

Video is most effective when used in short sequences to explain specific points. Don't be tempted to use video when a simpler technique will do – for example a 'talking head' on video is often less effective than you saying it yourself.

People are used to watching broadcast-quality television, and unless the video is of a very high standard it will lack credibility and the message will be lost. On the other hand, a video that is too gimmicky or humorous will only be remembered for its presentation and not for the message unless you recap or reinforce it in some way.

If you are flying to an engagement remember that some of the older airport security systems have been known to damage video tapes. Also remember that in the USA they use a different format to Europe.

Only use short clips; don't set a 30-minute programme going and sit back, then expect to keep your rapport with the audience. Make sure that each section you want to use is cued up in advance – do not spend time hunting through the tape in front of your audience.

Example

A head of department was running a series of team-building sessions with his department. In the first meeting he showed a short clip of a rugby match between England and New Zealand where a try was scored.

After that he did not have to say much about the merits of working as a team to convince them that teamwork was worthwhile.

Computers

These are best used when you want to demonstrate software, and in situations where you want participants to have 'hands-on' experience. But beware of keeping most people waiting for too long while others try something out.

Computers are most effective with very small groups, unless you have access to projection equipment.

Make sure you arrive in plenty of time to set up the equipment and test it thoroughly before your audience arrives. Computers are notorious for doing unexpected things at the last minute!

Objects as visual aids

There may be occasions when you want to show your audience an example of an object – educational equipment, examples of pupil's work or something else. This can serve a useful purpose if it adds to your presentation, so you should ask the same questions about its value as for any other visual aid. But in addition you should also consider:

Is it large enough for everyone to see?
Is it fragile or can it be passed around?
Would it be better shown as a photograph or diagram?

Then you can decide whether or not to use the object as part of your presentation.

Checklist

Using visual aids

Before you decide to use a visual aid you should ask the following questions:

Does it assist understanding?
Does it help to emphasize a point?
Is it really necessary?
Does it provide additional information which cannot be spoken?
Does it enhance or illustrate the spoken word and not confuse it?
Is it a good, clear, quality image?

If the answer to more than two of these is 'Yes', then the visual aid is likely to be a useful tool – but never accept 'No' as an answer to the last question!

Preparing good visuals

How often have you struggled to read cramped, over-full slides or illegible hand-written overhead foils? Have you ever had to watch fuzzy slides that are dirty with finger marks or with text over the edges of the screen? All these are problems which can be avoided at the production stage.

Scruffy hand-drawn visual aids do nothing to enhance a presentation and should be avoided. Only in exceptional circumstances are hand-written foils acceptable – when the producer has exceptional handwriting!

You must not compromise over clarity or quality. Poor visuals will detract from what you are saying and may do more harm than good.

You are unlikely to have the budget for a graphic artist to produce your visuals for you, but if you cannot have them made professionally, access to even basic equipment can produce some very good results. A simple DTP package is sufficient to produce clear text of a good size for overhead foils. This can then be printed straight on to special acetate or photocopied from paper onto photocopy film for foils. Word-processing packages will normally allow you to increase the size of the text. Providing it is well spaced and laid out, enlarging text on a photocopier is another solution if you have no other means.

Avoid the temptation to use too many different typefaces and sizes on one slide or foil. This makes them look 'busy' and can be confusing.

The guidelines in the next few paragraphs will help you to avoid some of the most common mistakes. If you want to take this topic further, there are courses available which can show you how to use other techniques to produce good visuals. The makers of overhead projector supplies are often willing to provide such help for only a nominal fee.

Position – favour the upper two-thirds of the slide.

Format – use the most suitable format: portrait or landscape. Be consistent and use the chosen format throughout any one presentation.

Lines and words – try to use no more than seven or eight lines of text on one slide. Try to keep to less than ten words on a line.

Letter size – on overhead foils use letters 8mm high or larger. Use larger letters for titles and sub-titles.

Format – text and headlines should be centred or ranged left.

Margins – leave a margin from the edge of the frame all round; this should be at least 2cm for overhead foils.

Spacing – leave gaps between lines to make key points stand out.

Simplify – when using maps or diagrams, simplify them for clarity. Where more complex information is to be shown, build up the information step by step by using overlays for overhead foils or a series of slides adding gradually to each successive slide.

Loading and using slides and foils

ACTIVITY

Think about presentations using visual aids which you have attended. What mistakes have you witnessed? Note them down here.

When you have read the rest of this chapter, come back to this list and consider how these problems could have been overcome. If there is no obvious solution, do you think the advantages outweighed the problems? In other words, was the presenter using the most appropriate visual aid and did it really enhance the presentation?

Slides

When using 35mm slides it is best to pre-load them into a carousel whenever possible. Use slides all in the same mounts – glass ones are best but more expensive than card-board. If the mounts are different, a slide projector with an auto-focus will have problems refocusing accurately. If it is a manual focus, you may find yourself having to adjust the focus whenever a different mount is used.

Check how to load (usually 'upside down and back to front') for the particular system you will use. Always make sure you run them through completely before you use them – it is very easy to get one the wrong way round. Whenever possible, run them through just before your presentation on the equipment and in the room you will use. This way you can make sure:

- the slides are still in position and the right way round;

- the equipment is focused correctly and the size is right for the screen;
- you know how to operate the equipment backwards as well as forwards.

This may mean arriving very early and checking your slides through before the first session of the day, or in a coffee break, but it is well worth the effort.

When you require a gap in the slides it is best to put in a 'blank'. This is a solid slide with nothing on it. It will stop you accidentally going on to a slide before you start talking about that topic, and it will save the horrible white glare of a gap in the slides.

Overhead projector foils

Try to organize your foils in frames or covers which will protect them and help you store them. 'Flip frames' protect the foil, allow you to store in a binder and do not have to be removed in use. Cardboard mounts hold the foils without creasing and can be laid on the projector accurately, but they are bulky to store. Both methods allow you to make notes around the slides for your own reference.

Try to make sure that you have two clear surfaces by the projector – one on which to put the foils ready for use, another to place foils when you have used them. This way you can pile your slides neatly in the correct order and all the same way up. Then when they have been used there is no danger of getting them muddled with the unused ones. If you want to use a foil more than once, copy it, don't rely on finding it again when it has been used. The additional preparation time can save a lot of embarrassment and confusion later.

If you are putting the foils onto the projector yourself you can easily control the pace. Some people prefer to switch the projector off between each foil as it is changed over. Provided you have all your foils ready in the correct order this is not usually necessary except where you change the subject and there is no foil for that topic.

You have probably seen presenters put on a foil then rapidly cover most of it with a sheet of paper. The problem with this is that you immediately begin to wonder what is beneath the paper. As it is gradually revealed the paper often becomes less secure and may eventually fall off too soon.

If you do not want to show the audience all the content of a foil in one go, there are better ways of doing it. The most effective is to prepare a series of foils, each one with something added to it. In this way the information builds up, the audience can concentrate on what you are saying and showing (not what is hidden) and you are less likely to make a mistake in showing too much too soon. This can be done as a series of separate foils or as overlays on the same frame.

When you put up a foil, give the audience time to take it in before you begin talking again. When you have finished, switch off the projector – a glaring white light is uncomfortable for the viewer, and keeping a foil up when you have moved on to another point is distracting.

Position

In the next chapter we will look at the layout of your venue, but where you stand, how you move and the position relative to your visual aid equipment is worth mentioning here.

While checking out your venue make sure that both you and the screen can be seen by all the audience. You may not want to stand still during your presentation. That is fine, but if you move around make sure that you do not walk between the projector and screen so that you block part of it.

If you have planned and prepared your visual aids correctly there should be no need to turn round and look at them after a quick glance to check the correct slide is up – face the audience, do *not* address the screen.

With slides you can stand to one side and use a pointer (a long stick will do if you do not have a pointer). This way you can still keep at least half-turned to the audience.

With overhead foils you can face the audience and point on the bed of the projector. Again, use a stick or pointer so you are not blocking the audience's view with your body.

Audio

Although we have mentioned the use of video as a visual aid we have not specifically talked about using sound as an aid. There is no reason why sound should not be used, and used well it can also add to a presentation. Sound can be used when:

- you want to hear live quotes from someone who cannot be present at the venue;
- you want to use music or sound effects as an example;
- you want to give examples of specific use of language.

You can probably think of other uses. Short extracts can change the pace, add another dimension and interest. But if you want to use sound you need to take account of all the guidelines given above for video. You must also take account of the quality of the sound and whether it can be heard adequately by all the audience. A tinny recording played by a miniature cassette player to a room of a hundred people can do little to enhance your presentation!

Don't let the technology take over

Remember that any aid is there to assist and enhance. Don't let it take over the presentation. Neither should you rely on it to give you the skills you need as a speaker.

It is tempting to plan your presentation around the visuals and then they take over. But you still need to talk to your audience. You can't just let them flounder, and if you let the technology drive you, you may leave the audience behind.

If something goes wrong with the equipment, think about the needs of your audience first – do not spend precious time fiddling with the equipment and forget about the audience. If the problem is not so obvious that it can be fixed in a minute or, if you are lucky, by a technician, then forget it. You should already have made contingency plans as we discussed in Chapter 2, so put them into operation and carry on.

ACTIVITY

Think about a presentation you might give, or one you have given in the past. Are (were) visual aids appropriate? If so write down what you would use (did/should have used) and why.

Type   **Reason**

When you are planning your presentation and you *do* wish to use visual aids, having to give yourself a good reason *why* is a useful discipline.

Having decided that you do wish to use a visual, use the guidelines earlier in this chapter to decide which to use and then sketch out your idea before you make it up into a slide, foil or flip chart.

Handouts – purpose and ideas for use

Like all supporting material, a good handout can be an asset, and a bad one is not worth producing. Handouts can be particularly useful when:

- you want the audience to take away some reference material;
- you have additional relevant material which time constraints prevent you using in your presentation;
- you want the audience to look at some visual materials but you have no projector to show it to the whole group;
- you want the audience to consider something (such as topics for discussion) which will be used later.

It is not normally a good idea to give out a transcript of your speech – the audience might just as well have stayed away and read it for themselves! Reminders of key points or topic headings might be useful; people can add their own notes to personalize it then.

Summary

The main types of visual aid are:

flip chart;
overhead projector;
35mm slide projector;
video;
computers.

Other aids can also be used – audio, objects and handouts.

Each has advantages and disadvantages and these should be taken into account when choosing the most appropriate medium for your needs.

Visual aids are powerful when they are used to benefit the presentation. To be effective they must be:

- well planned
- well prepared
- an enhancement to your words
- clear – not confusing.

Too many, poor quality or visuals of doubtful relevance do more harm than good. The same applies to handouts and audio.

Whichever aid you are using, make sure you have the sequence planned and know how to operate the equipment.

Used properly, visual aids can:

- arouse and maintain interest
- give variety in presentation
- save time – 'one picture is worth a thousand words'
- clarify difficult points
- give emphasis to points
- make use of another sense – the eyes as well as the ears
- help the memory – pictures can be remembered more easily than speech so, used in combination, words and pictures reinforce each other.

CHAPTER 4
Rehearsal and Final Preparation

Objectives

When you have completed this chapter you will:

- know why you should rehearse
- know how to use three different techniques for practising
- plan how others can help you
- be able to check your venue

Why rehearse?

ACTIVITY

Have you ever rehearsed a presentation?

If 'Yes', what did you gain from rehearsing?

If 'No', why did you think it unnecessary?

If you have already used rehearsal you are likely to see at least some value in it. If you do not think it necessary, we hope that it did not produce any problems, but any problems in your own presentation which did occur could probably have been overcome by rehearsal. This chapter will explain the benefits. There are four main areas where rehearsals will help:

- timing
- comfort
- writing your brief
- visual aids.

Timing

In Chapter 2 we talked about the importance of timing a presentation. It is frustrating both for presenter and audience to find that time has run out and only part of the topic has been covered. Unlike many classroom situations, you will not be able to get the group together again to finish off! Neither is it worthwhile to waste time by finishing far too early when you could have given the audience more useful information or examples (but not worthless padding just to fill the time).

Comfort

If you are familiar and comfortable with the material, you are going to be more confident. This will enable you to give a better presentation. Both you and the audience will benefit.

Writing your brief

By rehearsing you will find out if your notes really do help you. If they are too detailed you can trim them, if they are too brief you can add to them. Can you find your way around them easily – are they clear? Do you need to add some further memory-joggers? The rehearsal will give you time to do this in advance of the presentation. When you are on a platform it's too late to find out that your notes are inadequate.

Visual aids

A rehearsal will help you to ensure that you have all the visual aids you need and that they are in the right order to go with your notes. You can check if they fit in with the words and if they are helpful. You can also see if you want to add more or discard some.

Techniques for practising

A rehearsal is just what it says – an opportunity to go right through the whole presentation, including questions and visual aids whenever you can. There are three main ways you can do this:

1. Alone, you can record yourself on a tape or cassette and play it back.
2. Also alone, you can practise in front of a mirror, talk out loud at the pace you plan to use, and watch yourself.
3. With a friend or colleague, you can go through the presentation and ask for feedback.

Remember that when you listen to yourself you are hearing yourself through the bones in your head. Others hear your voice transmitted by air. The best way to hear yourself as others hear you is a recording. So, listening to yourself on tape has another advantage – you can hear and criticize your own voice. Is it a monotone, is it too high-pitched, is there no change of volume or pace? All these points could make it boring or difficult to listen to and can be improved. We will look at this again in Chapter 5.

ACTIVITY

Next time you ring someone up, listen carefully to the first few words they say, even just the first 'Hello'. What kind of mood are they in?

You can tell a lot about someone's mood from their tone of voice. If your voice is dull and flat it will not inspire your listeners; try to make your voice sound happy. Smile when you talk – it will come over in your voice. The rehearsal will help you to learn to do this.

While you are rehearsing, keep in mind the audience you are preparing for and what their expectations will be.

The purpose of rehearsal is to improve your presentation. If the results show that you have to do more work before the real thing, you should do it, so make sure you leave enough time to do this. If you go through the first rehearsal just before you give your presentation, it may give you some help but leave no time for implementing changes.

You should rehearse as often as you feel the need. The criteria are that you feel comfortable with the topic and you feel able to give the *outline* of the talk without any notes. But you should not learn it off by heart – you don't want to reel it off parrot-fashion and too many rehearsals and minor changes could make you go stale. You want to be able to focus on the audience but still think about what you are saying and sound interested and enthusiastic.

The words you use

Example

A physicist at a company research centre was asked to talk to a visiting group of school pupils about her job. She prepared the material and produced some professional visual aids.

The night before the talk she happened to mention it in conversation to her partner who said, 'I've always wanted to know what you really do – why don't you give the talk to me?'

She did, and afterwards he said it sounded good but he couldn't understand half of it! If *he* couldn't, how was she to expect a group of 12-year-olds to? So they went through the talk together and took out all the jargon, substituting simple explanations.

It meant a late night, but the talk went well the next day because it was appropriate for the audience.

All professions have their jargon – a convenient form of shorthand for talking with professional colleagues. But to others outside it does not make sense, and can sound as if you are trying to be superior. Educationalists talking to those outside their profession should be aware of this and, whenever in doubt, replace jargon with simple explanations. Using jargon is one of the most common faults of any professional talking to 'outsiders'.

Checking out the venue and equipment

Example

Two teachers were asked by a large manufacturing company to talk to their managers about a vocational course they had developed for 14- to 16-year-olds. The course required help from industry.

A training officer from the company visited the school to discuss arrangements with them. The teachers spent an hour with the training officer and discussed the target audience – there were to be 20 to 25 training and line managers. They also agreed the objectives and content for the talk. They asked about the venue and were told that it was a new conference centre with audio visual equipment provided. Everything sounded fine.

On the afternoon of the presentation the teachers arrived to prepare their session. After experiencing some difficulty in finding the new conference centre it turned out to be a converted warehouse next to the main production building of the factory. Very well appointed but vast! The audio visual kit was all there – a bank of 20 video screens, wall-mounted and geared to an audience of 200 not 20. But they did not want video and there were no technicians. They had brought 35mm slides. A slide projector was found, but no trolley. The position of the slide projector was governed by the position of the only power point outside the control room. In the event, the presentation was given with the projector perched on a stool on top of a coffee table, no sound system and the constant drone of factory machinery in the background.

In Chapter 1 we looked at the questions you should ask before you give a presentation. One section was about the venue. As the example above shows, you must take care to ask all the right questions and be sure you understand the same things by the answers as the other party.

If at all possible, try to visit the venue before the day of your presentation. If it is some distance away and you cannot visit, try to find out if any of your colleagues have been there and ask them about it. Also, ask the organizer or whoever has invited you for as much information as you can. If it is far enough away for you to travel there the night before, ask if you can have access on the evening you arrive. If all else fails, make sure you arrive in plenty of time on the day to check everything before the room fills up.

By getting to see the room in advance you can still have time to overcome any problems, or even move, before your talk.

The things you should be looking for when you check out your venue are:

- location and travel arrangements
- loading/unloading facilities
- seating arrangements
- location of equipment, power supplies and screens
- operation of equipment
- soundproofing and acoustics
- ventilation
- getting the 'feel' of the space.

Location and travel arrangements

You may need to find out how long it will take you to get there. If you are travelling by public transport, you need to know times (and reliability) of trains or buses and how far you may need to walk. If going by car, you need to know what arrangements there are for parking.

Arriving in a rush at the last minute is not going to help you to give a good presentation.

Loading/unloading facilities

If you have equipment, display materials or other things to carry, you should find out where you can load or unload to gain easy access. Many public venues have special loading areas which are not always obvious from the car parks. Even if there is no special loading area, you may be allowed to park temporarily somewhere for this purpose. It is worth asking the question if you have a lot to carry – it can save time and energy which are better put into the presentation.

Seating arrangements

Within the room you may be able to have the seats arranged as you wish. The most common arrangements are:

- theatre style
- classroom style
- boardroom style
- an open 'U'.

The best arrangement for your presentation depends on the numbers and your preferred presentation style. It may also be dictated by the constraints of the room. A traditional lecture theatre can only be this style as the seats are fixed. A boardroom style is not appropriate for more than about 20 people, and so on.

ACTIVITY

Think about presentations you have given or attended and the way the room was laid out. For each of the styles listed, make a note of the ideal numbers and the most appropriate style of presentation to use with this layout.

Theatre style
Numbers:
Most appropriate for:

Classroom style
Numbers:
Most appropriate for:

Boardroom style
Numbers:
Most appropriate for:

Open 'U'
Numbers:
Most appropriate for:

You can use this as a quick checklist when you are planning a presentation.

You will also need to take account of the shape of the room and visibility; see the section on 'See and be seen' later in this chapter.

Location of equipment, power supplies and screens

You need to find out where the equipment is to be placed and where the nearest power supply is. The relative positions of equipment and power are especially important if you are providing your own equipment – it is more likely the venue will already have this organized if they are supplying their own equipment.

You may need more than one socket or an extension lead. Many experienced presenters carry an extension lead with multiple sockets with them just in case!

If you are giving a presentation abroad, you may even need adaptors for the power supply to operate your equipment. In these cases it is better to ask the venue to supply equipment. Also, remember that the United States uses a different TV and video system to Europe. If you must use video, you will need to get it transferred.

If you want to use projection you will need a screen or plain, light coloured, non-reflective wall. It must be in a position which the audience can see. See the section on 'See and be seen' later in this chapter.

Operation of equipment

Example

A teacher had been asked to give a talk to a group of company personnel about a project his pupils had undertaken for the local council. The purpose was to give a case study of school pupils preparing for work. The teacher had a number of good slide photographs of the pupils doing the project work and of some of their completed projects. The presentation was to take place in a local hotel during the first session after morning coffee.

The teacher left school after assembly and arrived just before the coffee break. She asked to see the room, and as soon as the delegates went to coffee, put her carousel of photographs on the projector to run through them. The projector had been set up by the hotel but not used that day. It had a remote control which the teacher was familiar with. But when she tried it, she could only get the slides to run backwards! Help from the company trainer failed to solve the problem.

The trainer went out into the lobby and made sure everyone had another cup of coffee, while the teacher rapidly reorganized her slides into reverse order.

The example shows the value of arriving in time and checking things out – plus some lateral thinking to find a quick solution.

If you are taking your own equipment, make sure it is still working when you get there. It is a good idea to take a spare bulb and fuse – and know how to fit them.

If you are using equipment at the venue make sure you know how to switch it on and off (not always as easy as it sounds) and how to focus and change slides. If there is a remote control this may operate backwards and forwards; make sure you check out which is which.

Soundproofing and acoustics

You may not always have the option of selecting the venue for its sound qualities, but at least if you know how noisy it is you can plan accordingly. For example, presentations in schools during the working day can be difficult during break times due to the noise from playgrounds – so plan your breaks to coincide.

One room may be noisier than another due to the proximity of a main road – see if you can move rooms.

If you have a quiet voice and the acoustics are bad or the room noisy, see if you can use a microphone – and make sure you know how it works.

Ventilation

A hot stuffy room will send your audience to sleep. A room which may be comfortable when empty can be too hot when full. See if you can control the heating accordingly. If the room has the luxury of air conditioning – and most modern hotel rooms do – find out how it works and if you can control it from inside your room.

A room which is too cold will make the audience uncomfortable and they will lose concentration. Again, see what you can do to control the temperature.

If you cannot control the temperature then try to warn the audience and suggest they come in layers they can alter as appropriate. One international training company that holds seminars in hotels all over the world always puts this in its joining instructions, and it has proved to be well received by their clients.

How you fit in

Get the 'feel' of the space. If you have time, try to walk around the room, get the impression of how large it is and how the audience will see you. How close will they be to you?

If you are going to be called from the body of the room onto a platform, how far is it and which way will you get there?

Checklist

Equipment

What can the organizers or venue supply?
Make/model of any equipment.
Type of carousel or slides.
Stand.
Power supply (some factories do not have normal 13 amp power).
Screen.
Spare bulb, fuses, etc.
Technical support – is there someone who can set up the equipment and explain its operation to you?
Check it is working correctly before the audience arrives.
If using video, cue it up.

See and be seen

As we have already said, it is unusual for you to have complete control over the venue for your presentations. More often than not you will have to make the best of what you are given, but if you do have a choice of venue or layout, consider visibility: can the audience see you and your visual aids, and can you see them?

Avoid rooms with low ceilings. A low ceiling may make projection difficult. It can also make the room claustrophobic when it is full.

Try to ensure that the screen is above the head level of the audience (unless the room has tiered seating like a lecture theatre). The front row of seats should be about the same distance from the screen as twice the height from the floor to the bottom of the screen.

Viewing angles will also affect what the audience can see. Seats at some parts of the room will have a poor view even if the screen and speaker are above their head height. Seats at angles of less than 60 degrees from the front centre will have a poor view.

You will also need to take account of any pillars or other obstructions which protrude into the room. If you have time to walk around the room and check visibility, you could then move or remove seats from the affected areas.

Overcoming problems

Below is a checklist of some of the most common problems which you may encounter and some suggested solutions. These may not be the only answers, so add your own where you can and use this as a 'troubleshooting checklist' if you need it.

Checklist

Solving problems

Problem	Possible solution
Projector does not work	Check plug, fuse and bulb.
Power point too far away	Carry an extension lead with you. Can you turn the audience to face the projector in another position?
No power point available	Have an alternative to your visual aids.
Room does not black out	Can you move rooms? Can the projector and screen be moved out of the glare?
Room is too large	Can you change rooms? Can you rearrange seating to make it look better? Are there any screens or display boards you can use to partition it?
The room is too small	Can you move rooms? Can you remove any furniture?

	Can you rearrange seats to make better use of the space?
The room is too noisy	Can you move rooms?
	Can you rearrange the seats to help the audience hear you better?
	Can you get a PA system?
	Can you have the noise stopped or reduced while you talk?

If you are used to giving presentations, you learn by every problem you have and from every time something goes wrong. As a result, many experienced presenters carry around with them a 'toolkit' of items which they can use to solve problems. Below is the contents of one such kit:

- extension lead and four-gang socket
- fuses in variety of sizes
- electrical screwdriver
- spare bulb for projector (you need to know which projector!)
- Blu-Tack
- flip chart
- pens for flip chart and white boards
- blank overhead foils.

You may not want or need all these, or you may want to make up your own list from your own experiences.

Checklist

The venue

- What is the size of the room?
- Is the room well ventilated? Can you control the temperature?
- Is the room soundproof?
- What are the room acoustics like?
- What are the seating arrangements?
- Are there any surfaces to lean and write on?
- Where are the power points? Do you need an extension lead?

Is there a stand/trolley for the projector?
Can everyone see you clearly?
Can you position the screen for everyone to see?
Can you reach light switches if you need to turn them off?
Is there car parking for loading and unloading?
How do you get there and how long will it take?

Summary

Rehearsals will:

- help you to familiarize yourself with the material for your presentation;
- give you confidence;
- check that all the material is logical and fits together;
- help you to hear yourself as others hear you;
- improve the use of changes in tone and pace;
- help you keep to time.

You can practice alone or with the help of others.

Visit the venue in advance and go through the checklists. Ensure the room and seating arrangements are suitable.

Make sure you are familiar with the equipment available and it operates correctly. Use the checklists to do this.

CHAPTER 5

Giving the Presentation: I

Objectives

When you have completed this chapter you will:

- know what makes an audience take notice of your presentation
- know how to present a good image of yourself
- make the best use of your voice
- know at least two techniques for overcoming nerves.

Getting past the barrier

If you can describe the written word as a monochrome, single-input form of passing a message, a presentation should be a multi-colour, multi-track input. This means that when you are giving a presentation there are a number of ways in which you are communicating; your voice is only one of them. In this chapter we will look at the different facets of that communication.

As the brain is divided up into a number of different areas, so is the way it receives messages. The first reaction to any message is emotional, whether we want it to be or not. The brain receives messages about the speaker before he or she even opens their mouth. These messages will trigger that immediate emotional response – the 'feeling' we often experience when we meet someone for the first time.

We could describe the intellect as being hidden behind the emotional barrier. This emotional response is unconscious, and the listener rarely controls it. The intellect is a conscious and controllable response.

So, before we can persuade or inform the listener with our words we have to make them want to listen. If the emotional barrier closes you out, the sensory inputs to the intellect are unlikely to make an impact. If you appear boring, anxious or insincere, your words may not even reach the intended destination. They will be turned off by the poor initial response. The content of what you say can also be blocked by inconsistent verbal and visual messages.

The trick, then, is to make the audience want to listen. This is not as difficult as it sounds. You need to make them trust in you, believe in your ability and be open to your input.

ACTIVITY

Stand up, hold your hands clasped in front of you and look down at them. Try saying out loud: 'I am really pleased to be here'.

If you can get someone to watch while you do this and comment on the way it made them feel, that would be even better.

Did it sound to you as if you really meant what you were saying? If someone was watching you, what was their reaction? The chances are that you did not sound pleased or enthusiastic, and that your words may have said one thing to your watcher while your body said another. This is confusing and disorienting.

People see you as 50 to 57 per cent total image (appearance and body language), 38 to 40 per cent how you deliver your message (voice, tone and so on), and only 5 to 10 per cent what you actually say. The rest of this chapter will explain ways you can improve your presentation technique and get past the first barrier.

First impressions

The first minute will tell your audience enough about you to set their expectations for the whole presentation. You never get a second chance at making a first impression – so the impression you give must be right.

Appearance

Example

> In the 1980s a trade union official was asked by a teacher to talk to a group of 14- and 15-year-olds as part of a course on industrial history.
>
> He was introduced briefly by the class teacher who then suggested that he explain his role more fully. He was part-way through an explanation of his work when one of the pupils butted in scathingly, 'You're not a trade unionist – you're wearing a suit!' The visitor went on to explain that he was not in his working environment and was here to represent his colleagues, so he felt it appropriate to come smartly dressed.

Look smart and professional. The keyword is 'appropriate' – dress in a manner appropriate to your position. Think about how the audience will view you. If in doubt, be conservative and always groom and dress up, rather than down. Think about your dress consciously for a presentation, not just according to habit. Be aware of what is right for you as well as the audience and situation. You may not be used to dressing formally, but in certain situations an over-casual appearance can say to your audience, 'This person is treating us casually'. So, find a good compromise where you will feel comfortable but the audience will also feel comfortable and be able to identify with you.

Try to avoid wearing something brand new. It may not be comfortable and this could distract you. It may also behave unexpectedly, like a skirt which rides up or is too short when you sit down (remember you may well be on a platform above the first few rows of the audience), a shirt which has a collar too tight or a jacket which you cannot unbutton easily if you get too warm. Avoid wearing anything distracting such as a very bold tie or jewellery which rattles if you move. It can divert the audience's attention.

Your hair and face are most important – that's where people will look when you are talking to them.

Get feedback from friends and colleagues if you are unsure; ask their opinions or ask for some guidance from whoever has asked you to speak. Also, look at others who give presentations and ask yourself what messages their dress and grooming give you.

Body language

This is a whole subject in itself and we will only give some brief guidelines here; however, it is important and you need to consider it.

ACTIVITY

Stand up and slump your posture so that your shoulders are hunched forward, your head down and your arms crossed across your chest. Now try to walk forward. Is it easy to stride out or walk quickly?

Do you think you look positive or confident?

The chances are you'll be thinking, 'Of course not!'. But it is amazing how often people walk onto a platform in this way. If you walk boldly and confidently, the audience will get the feeling that you are confident in your topic and will have confidence in you.

When you stand still, again your body will send out a message. Stand upright – not like a puppet pulled tight on a string but with your head up and body straight. It will help you to make visual contact with your audience and to breathe better; this in turn will help your voice. Avoid going back on one hip, folding your arms or clasping your hands in front of you like a fig leaf. All these gestures will convey insecurity or lack of interest. Keep your weight forward: this will direct your energy forward and make you look ready for action. An open body posture and smiles are welcoming – not a fixed grin or put-on smile, but a natural, relaxed facial expression.

Be yourself: do not try to eradicate movement and gestures. Movement is dynamic and can add to your delivery. Again, this should be used in moderation. If you know you have any annoying habits, it is worth working on trying to stop these.

ACTIVITY

Whenever you give a presentation, ask a friend to watch and make a note of one or two habits which they find irritating. Then, before your next presentation, work on getting rid of these. Don't try to do too much at once, or you'll spend more time worrying about the habit than about your presentation.

Some habits you can overcome by removing the source. For example, if you have a habit of jangling the loose change in your pocket – empty your pockets; if you fiddle with your earrings – take them off.

Eye contact

Treat your audience as a number of individuals, not just one huge mass. Make eye contact as they walk into the room or as you walk onto the platform, not just during the presentation.

ACTIVITY

Find an empty room with a number of chairs laid out. Stick a picture of a face or a different coloured piece of paper on the back of each chair. Stand in front of the chairs as if you were giving a presentation and look at every 'face' for four to five seconds. When you have done this once, do it again while you talk. Do not go along row by row in order – move your eyes around, but hold each look for 5 seconds.

Visual connection is the best way of establishing contact with your audience and involving them in your presentation. Involve as many as possible as early as possible, but remember the four to five seconds rule. If your eyes are constantly darting around the room, this makes you look nervous and 'shifty', which will make the audience feel that you are not believable.

While you are talking, look at the audience to see how they are reacting to you. Respond to them: if they are looking bored, speed up or use some visuals to change the flow; if they are looking lost, slow down and use some examples to explain or summarize key points.

Movement

Moving while you talk can help to make you look energetic and enthusiastic. If you feel comfortable moving about in front of your audience, you should do it. But be careful of the following pitfalls:

- don't look like a caged animal pacing up and down;
- don't walk in front of the projector so you block the image;
- don't go away from your notes if you are not confident enough that you can work without them for a while.

Even if you don't want to move, simple gestures are accept-able and if they come naturally to you, they will enhance your presentation. Again use in moderation – you don't want to look as if you are giving your talk in semaphore.

If there is a physical barrier between you and the audience, it may create an emotional one. If you can, try to avoid standing behind a lectern or table. If you do not want to go too far from your notes, stand at the side, or take the notes with you.

Using the voice

Again, much has been written and said about using and improving your voice. We will just touch on the subject here and give you some guidelines which you may find useful.

The voice is the instrument by which you will communicate the information you want to give. The figures we gave earlier in this chapter for how people 'see' you show that over a third of your communication is by the *way* you say something. Your voice is the one piece of equipment which is within your control; with thought and practice you can make your voice work better for you.

The basic process of speech is that sounds are made by forcing air across the vocal chords which vibrate to make a noise. This noise can be varied by altering the amount and speed of air used. This is done by the use of the muscles in the chest and the diaphragm. The more delicate muscle movements in the face, tongue, mouth and throat then 'tune' the sounds into speech. This means that the way you breathe has the most effect on your voice. Breathing steadily and deeply will help give a firm, steady voice.

Many people find it difficult to talk loudly and clearly, and they may try to shout which only results in damage and voice loss. This is often accentuated by the stress of giving the presentation. Try to make your voice deeper (this is especially difficult but important for anyone with a high-pitched voice). This can be helped by breathing from deeper in your diaphragm and slowing down the pace of your delivery. Slowing down will also encourage you to pronounce your words more deliberately and so more clearly. Clear pronunciation is vital for the audience to hear what you say.

There are a number of exercises you can do to improve the use of your voice, and if you feel this would help, you should read some specialist information on the subject.

Stress and the voice

Few speakers can truly say they feel no stress when they are giving a presentation. Stress brings on tension and this will affect the voice. The effects of stress include:

- quick and shallow breathing, which makes it difficult to control the volume of the voice;
- muscle tension, which impairs breathing and prevents correct formation of words;
- an increase in adrenaline which speeds up the pace of delivery; this makes words difficult to pronounce clearly;
- the mouth drying up, making it difficult to use the tongue and throat effectively.

These effects can be overcome; the following checklist gives some hints on how to do this.

Checklist

Stress and the voice

Be prepared – if you know your material well, the presentation will be less stressful.

Know your opening. The first two minutes are the most stressful time, so be able to recite the first two minutes without your notes, whatever happens. If you get through this successfully it will give you confidence.

Relax the muscles in your upper body, arms and neck just before you start. Take slow deep breaths and gently move the shoulders and neck to relieve tension.

Have a glass of water handy and take a small drink as, or just before, you stand up to speak.

Overcoming nerves

ACTIVITY

Take a piece of paper and make a list in two columns of what you like and dislike about making presentations.

Think about and add reasons for *why* you have these likes and dislikes.

Look at the reasons for your likes. Can you build on these in any way? If so, think how you can make the best of your likes and jot these ideas down.

Look at the reasons for your dislikes. Are any of them because you are not in control or might get it wrong? If these are the reasons, there are ways to overcome the problems. We will come back to this list soon.

Anxiety is frequently brought about by fear of failing. If you can be in control of your presentation, you can be in control of its success. Pilots are not afraid of flying – why? Because they are in control, they know what to do if the situation changes, and they can control it.

Anxieties can be divided into four areas of control:

- managing the material
- managing the resources
- managing the audience
- managing yourself.

ACTIVITY

Go back to the list of dislikes you made in the previous activity.

For each one, note next to it which of the four areas of management (listed above) applies.

Some of these problems have already been addressed in earlier chapters in this book. For example, 'managing the materials' can be controlled by good planning. So, for each of the dislikes, you should be able to add a solution. A few areas are still to be explained; as you read the rest of this chapter and Chapter 6 you should be able to complete your list.

Controlling yourself

Even the most experienced professional may experience some anxiety at times, but this does not mean that they will give a poor performance. A small amount of anxiety can produce the adrenaline which you need to give a powerful performance.

By knowing you are well-prepared and have checked out your material and equipment, there are fewer things to go wrong – so you are less likely to fail.

Positive thinking is a very powerful tool. As you prepare and when you stand up to speak, imagine yourself doing well – imagine the smiles of appreciation and applause of the audience. This will set your expectations in a positive frame of mind and this will make it easier for you to do well.

To help you to relax and control yourself, the following checklist may be helpful.

Checklist

Controlling yourself

Take a few deep breaths. This slows down your rate of breathing and your pulse.

By slowing down your breathing you can control the pace of your delivery.

Think to yourself, 'I am going to enjoy this. I've done my preparation and I know what I'm talking about'.

Show conviction; believe in what you have to say.

Most of the audience have come to hear what you have to say, and the majority will want to like you and listen attentively.

Unless the audience is highly sadistic, they would rather see you enjoy this than sit through a nervous breakdown!

Use your voice well – see the checklist on stress and the voice earlier in this chapter.

You are almost certainly better than you think. Trust yourself and the audience will trust you.

Summary

First impressions will tell the audience a lot about you. Only 5 to 10 per cent of your message is given by what you say. Appearance, body language and *how* you speak make up the rest of the message.

Dress appropriately, walk and speak confidently. Make good use of eye contact. Move about if you want to.

Be natural: by being yourself you can make the contact you need to get past the emotional barriers to the intellect. The intention is to seem as if you are having a conversation with the audience, not talking at them. Through your own confidence, how you present yourself, eye contact and by involving your audience, you will get them to trust you and trust is the basis of belief.

Overcome nerves by:

- managing your material
- managing your resources
- managing your audience
- managing yourself.

Positive thinking will help you to do well.

CHAPTER 6
Giving the Presentation: 2

Objectives

When you have completed this chapter you will:

- know how to open a presentation effectively to gain attention
- know techniques for keeping the attention of your audience
- know how to work through your presentation in a structured way even if the situation changes
- be able to handle questions and discussion
- be able to close the presentation effectively.

Beginning

Put your notes where you can see them easily – there is no point in trying to hide them. Also, make sure you can see the time easily; if there is no clock in view take off your watch and put it where you can easily glance at it without being too obvious.

Starting off is always the most difficult. After the shock of the first few moments of hearing your voice, you will be surprised how quickly you settle into the content of your talk.

Before you get down to the content of your talk, you may need to introduce yourself. This will depend on whether or not you have been properly introduced by the chairman or host. You should also outline the presentation at this stage by explaining your objectives, what you are going to talk about (headings only), give an idea of what other materials are available (so the audience knows whether to take notes or not) and how you wish to take questions, if at all. The objectives and key headings could also be shown as a visual to reinforce the points.

ACTIVITY

Think about a presentation you have given or will soon be giving. Write an opening for it. Read it out loud and time it.

Now check your opening against the list below. The answers to the first seven questions should be 'Yes', and the last one 'No', otherwise it can be improved. If it is too long you may have 'lost' your audience before you have really begun. You would then have to work twice as hard to win them back.

Does your opening:

1. Explain who are you and what experience you have to speak on this topic?
2. Tell the audience the objectives for the presentation?
3. Outline the topics that will be covered?
4. Explain if there are handouts or other materials to take away?
5. Say how long will it last?
6. Tell them if there will be an opportunity for questions?
7. If so, when and in what form?
8. Last longer than three minutes (or about 10 per cent of the total time)?

The next step is to grab the attention of the audience as you move into the main body of the talk. Open with a statement which will make your audience sit up and take notice. This must only be a maximum of two or three minutes long. For example:

'A survey published last week shows that 75 per cent of employers do not know what the Certificate of Personal Achievement can tell them about a potential employee.'

'NCVQ has endorsed the Young Enterprise programme as an ideal activity to provide evidence for GNVQ and NVQ. My presentation this afternoon will explain how you can take advantage of that for your pupils.'

'Teachers spend 25 per cent of their time in non-productive activity in the classroom. I intend to show you how you can reduce that to almost nil!'

To create impact, you may choose to give this opening statement before your general introduction. For example:

'Eighty-five per cent of teachers have never received any training on financial management – this results in up to 20 per cent of school budgets being wasted unnecessarily. This evening I will show you techniques which can help you to reduce this waste to nil! My name is Jean Harris, my experience has been in both the education sector and local authority, managing budgets of up to £150,000, then successfully managing a small business of my own in the private sector.

'My objectives this evening are. . .'

. . . and so on.

The opening statement needs to make the audience believe that the presentation will be of interest to them and show them that they can trust you. Remembering what we said in Chapter 5, this will be a combination of your appearance, body language and voice as well as what you say. In these first few minutes they will decide:

- if they are interested;
- if they need to listen;
- if they are going to believe what the presenter has to say;
- if the presenter is the right person to be addressing them.

If you do not make a favourable impression on your audience in these first few minutes the success of the presentation will be damaged at best, prevented at worst.

It can also be a good idea to involve your audience at a very early stage. Ask them a rhetorical question. In the first example above you could have said, 'Did you know...', or even ask for a show of hands:

> 'How many of you here today have *never* had a problem with your marking schedules?'

You should then be prepared to pick up and comment on the response:

> 'Judging by that response, almost all of you will benefit from our first activity, and I hope that the rest will be prepared to share their experience to help us all.'

It is not normally a good idea to use a joke as an ice-breaker – very few people are really good joke tellers and if it falls flat it sets the tone for the rest of the presentation. But a dramatic story or anecdote can be a powerful opening.

Keeping attention

The old saying, 'Variety is the spice of life' could also be said to be true of presentations. Not a constant round of tricks and gimmicks, but changes of pace and medium, and examples to illustrate can help to maintain attention. Various studies on attention spans have produced different figures, but it is generally thought that the attention span of even the most intellectually capable tails off after seven or eight minutes. If this is put on a graph, it shows an initial peak gradually tailing away to seven minutes, then dropping off very rapidly. Your aim is to raise the attention to the peaks again before it hits the troughs. You can do this by introducing change before it tails off too far, by adding interesting examples to the content, changing the media and using variations in tone, pace and pitch of your voice.

Content

Don't bombard your audience with a constant stream of facts and figures. Break it up with examples and anecdotes.

If you are covering a detailed or complex topic, stop at the end of each key area and summarize. A visual at this point could be very useful. If appropriate, you may choose to ask your audience if they need any clarification before you move on.

Use humour to make it enjoyable, but use it carefully. People will remember things they have enjoyed. This is where you make use of your 'story diary' we suggested in Chapter 2. Include amusing stories and anecdotes to illustrate points or develop ideas. Again, set-piece jokes are not the best idea – humour is personal and what is funny to one person may offend others, but a story about something that happened to you or a colleague can be very successful.

Media

In Chapter 3 we talked about the production of visual aids. As well as having the benefit of presenting the information in a different way, and thus catering for people with different preferred learning styles, a change of medium can raise the attention of the audience.

Using more than one medium can increase this further, but the logistics of this may not be easy, and too many changes can disorientate or irritate the audience. There are no hard and fast rules about this; it depends on the length of the presentation, so use your judgement.

The voice

Use your voice to change the delivery. Changes of pace and volume help to keep the audience interested. When you want to say something important, slow the pace down, even talk quieter so they have to listen carefully – but not so quietly you cannot be heard! When you turn the volume down remember to speak especially clearly.

The tone of your voice can also convey messages. Use confiding tones when you want to get across a particularly important point. You can also use pauses very effectively. A brief silence (as much as five to eight seconds) can make the audience sit up and take notice before a key statement. People will look up – they may even think you've forgotten your words – and then they will be listening.

Checklist

Keeping attention
Involve your audience.
Vary the pace of your delivery.
Use your voice to change tone and volume.
Use visual aids to add another dimension.
Use other media to add variety where appropriate.
Give the audience a comfort or stretch break during long
    sessions.

Making adjustments

Time constraints

You may have to adjust the length of your presentation at the last minute because the meeting is running late, or as you go along because some parts took longer than you had planned.

It is in these cases where the technique of highlighting your notes into 'musts, shoulds and coulds' is most helpful. If you have to save time, you can miss out all the 'coulds' and some of the 'shoulds'. If you have highlighted your notes to colour code them, this will be easier.

Time expands

If you finish early you can add back the 'shoulds' and 'coulds', or if you have covered all you had in your notes, you can add some additional anecdotes. It is always useful to have a few extra stories or examples available. You can also usefully go back to the outline you gave at the beginning and recap with a brief summary of the key points (see also 'Finale' in the next section).

It is not normally a problem to finish early – unlike many lessons where you have to keep the pupils occupied until the bell. A mature audience will appreciate that you have covered all that the topic required and be grateful not to be kept unnecessarily.

Forgetting your words

If you forget what you are going to say or lose your place in your notes, you need to buy time. You can do this by summarizing or recapping the last few key points or the last topic. This should give you time to gather your thoughts and find where to go next. But if your notes are planned properly to help you and you have rehearsed well, this is unlikely to happen.

Dealing with questions and discussion

Fear of questions

ACTIVITY

If you have any concerns about handling questions, make a list on a piece of paper of your top five fears about answering questions.

Remembering the list of things to manage in Chapter 5 – yourself, your material, the audience, your resources – label each of your fears.

Things which you can manage are the easiest to overcome. Your planning and preparation should include a list of the questions you are likely to get, so you can research the answers in advance. This will overcome the 'materials fears'. Similarly, planning and preparation should overcome the 'resources' fears. The hints we have given on overcoming nerves in Chapter 5 should help you to overcome the 'yourself' fears.

The rest of this section will give you tips on managing the audience. You can plan and prepare as well as is possible, but when you are interacting with the audience there is always a degree of uncertainty.

You will need to maintain control of time and structure. For this reason, it is normally best to ask the audience to keep questions to the end. A long discussion in the middle of the presentation can make you lose the train of your thoughts and can throw out your planned timings very badly.

Avoiding impromptu questions

If you are in doubt about your ability to think on your feet or to handle questions, defer questions until after the presentation by saying you will be willing to talk individually to people over coffee. If this is not practical, ask for written questions which you can reply to individually. Sometimes in conferences where there is a panel, at the end members of the audience are invited to present written questions in the break before the panel.

Questions to the audience

We have already mentioned that asking the audience questions is a way of involving them in your presentation. They could lead to having to deal with the unexpected, so unless you do not actually allow a response, you should be prepared to react to the replies. However, questions to the audience can be a valuable tool. They can:

- check the knowledge level of the audience about certain topics;
- introduce variety and change of pace;
- arouse the interest of the audience;
- build up a rapport with the audience;
- check understanding of what has been said;
- allay any doubts that the audience may otherwise take away with them;
- discover how much interest has been generated;

- encourage the audience to think about what you have said;
- stimulate discussion.

The two main types of question – open and closed – have different uses. Closed questions are the easiest to use. They have a definite answer and do not encourage discussion. An example of a closed question is: 'Are you involved in the delivery of Key Stage one in English?'

Open questions will lead to comment and discussion, so only use these when you feel able to deal with some discussion. Open questions usually start with words like what, why, when, where or who. An example would be: 'At what stage should you introduce presentational skills?'

Whether open or closed, be careful to make your questions clear and unambiguous, and only ask one question at a time. Questions are best used to clarify understanding; they should not confuse.

Questions to the speaker

You can satisfy the needs or interests of individuals in the audience by allowing them to ask you questions. Exactly how you handle the taking of questions will depend on the size of audience and whether or not you have a chairperson or host to take and direct the questions. When you are handling questions directly by yourself, you will need to watch for hands going up and make a note of the order to try to be fair in satisfying needs.

Questions to the speaker can:

- help the audience clarify points they do not understand;
- test the presenter's credibility as an expert;
- gain more information on points raised;
- express opinions or concerns.

When a question has been asked, don't rush in with an answer. Take your time and ask yourself:

Have I understood the question? If not, ask for it to be repeated.

Has the group understood the question or should I para-phrase it back to the questioner to be sure?

Why is he or she asking – does he or she want information or debate?

Is it relevant to the topic in hand? If not, should I defer it to a private discussion later?

How far should I go in my reply to benefit the group (they may not all be interested)? How much time should I spend on one person?

Can I usefully pass it back to the group to enlist their help and interest?

Dealing with difficult questions

Sometimes you will be asked difficult questions. This may be because the questioner genuinely wants to know, but some-times they are trying to cause mischief. Try to decide which it is, but at first always treat it as a genuine question.

If you do not know the answer, say so; don't try to cover up – the audience will guess. Say that you don't know but you are willing to find out, and ask the questioner if he or she would like to leave their card or address for you to con-tact them later. You may choose to pass it on to a colleague if there is a panel. You need to be sure they will be able to respond: don't drop your colleagues in it! A general request to the rest of the audience can be a bit risky and is probably best avoided.

If a question or statement is absurdly simple, don't cast scorn – it could be genuine. Give a simple direct answer or refer tactfully to materials in the handout or, if you suspect they are being mischievous, ask the questioner, 'Could you explain exactly why you think that?'

If a question is long and rambling and you suspect that the speaker just wants to make a statement, you can respond with something like, 'I think the question you are asking is ...', then state your own question which you then answer. Do not say, 'I'm not sure what question you are asking' or they will take the opportunity to give it all over again!

If a question is irrelevant, give a brief but firm answer such as, 'This is an interesting point but...' and offer to discuss it further afterwards.

If the question invites detailed discussion on issues obviously only of interest to the questioner, give as brief an answer as you can and offer to discuss it afterwards. If they insist and are obviously being mischievous, use peer-group pressure: ask the rest of the audience if they wish you to continue or close it now.

If a question is provocative, don't get involved in a one-to-one argument. Be assertive, neither aggressive nor submissive, and state that the question is not relevant or helpful. If the questioner insists on pursuing it, offer to talk afterwards, and, if necessary, again you could use peer-group pressure. You do not want to lose the sympathy of your audience by putting someone down rudely or unkindly, but chances are most of them will not want it continued, so by involving them you gain their help and sympathy.

If a question has a number of parts, write them down (it is advisable to make notes as questions are asked anyway) and deal with one part at a time.

If a question is obviously designed to mislead, confuse or undermine you, ask the questioner what his or her hidden agenda is.

If you know the answer but your mind has gone blank, relax, take a few deep breaths and think for a few moments. If it still does not come, say what has happened, make a note of it and come back to it later – something else is bound to trigger the answer when you are not trying to think of it.

Checklist

Question management

Anticipate questions; plan by listing all the points which may want clarification and other possible questions you can think of, then prepare material to cover these.

Tell the audience when you will be taking questions. Don't let questions rule the presentation.

Know your topic well and be well prepared.

Listen carefully, make notes and give the questioner time to finish.

In your answers be brief, courteous and to the point.

If the question is technical or unclear, 'translate' or paraphrase it for the benefit of the group.

Restate the question if the all the audience may not have heard it.

Expect some difficult questions and learn the techniques for dealing with them.

Do not get involved in discussions only of interest to the questioner; be assertive.

Keep eye contact with the questioner where possible; break it when enlisting the help of the group.

Give positive responses wherever possible. If the question requires a negative response, try to end on a positive note.

Remember that questions are your opportunity to add credibility to your presentation.

Finale

The role of the summary is to bring the presentation to a recognizable conclusion, reiterate and reinforce the main points and create a positive lasting impression. It signals to the audience that they have been given all the information, and you have the chance to draw it to a positive conclusion. The last thing the audience hears will be what they remember most clearly. You can remind people of your major points and reinforce them in their minds. You can also take the opportunity to make strong recommendations based on your key points.

If you finish on a decisive and positive note your ideas will be remembered in the same way. When questions follow the summary they can detract from your own final words, especially if they have been difficult. For this reason it is sometimes a good idea to have a statement to give after questions; this may repeat some of the summary, but should include the most positive points.

A strong summary is your parting shot – it is usually underrated by inexperienced presenters, but never dismiss its value and the lasting impression it can give.

Checklist

A good summary

A summary should include:

- a recap of the main theme
- emphasis on the main points
- a recommendation or proposal for decisions or actions, ie, what to do next
- positive statements
- a thank you for listening.

Be positive and upbeat; the summary should not include any new ideas or downbeat and negative tones.

Summary

Begin by explaining who you are, what your presentation will cover and how it is structured. Use the checklist for beginning the presentation.

During the main body of your presentation, check on the reactions of your audience and adapt to their needs. Use techniques listed in the checklist for maintaining their attention.

If you agree to take questions, deal with questioners courteously. Be assertive and take account of the needs of the whole audience. Use the question management checklist to guide you.

Finish by drawing together key themes; the summary checklist can guide you. Be positive and upbeat in your conclusions.

CHAPTER 7
Putting it all Together

Objective

When you have completed this chapter you will:

- understand how to plan, prepare and present an effective presentation.

Introduction

The purpose of this chapter is to bring together the key points from all the preceding chapters. It will reinforce what you have learned so far, and you can use it in future to refresh your memory when you have to give a presentation.

A presentation is a situation where someone gives information to an audience, large or small. This communication can be given in a number of ways, but it is primarily verbal, and the main flow is from presenter to audience.

The main reason for a poor presentation is that it has not been well prepared. This leads to inappropriate material, poor timing, poor visual aids, and lack of variety and interest. Good preparation is the key to a good presentation.

Know your audience and purpose

When first approached

When you are first asked to give a presentation you should ask questions to clarify the purpose of the event and to learn more about the audience. Questions to ask should include:

Date:
>   What day and at what time is it?

Audience:
>   Who is the audience (age, subject knowledge, etc)?
>   Why are they coming?
>   What do they expect to get out of it?
>   How many people do you expect to attend?

Event:
>   What is the aim of the event?
>   What are the desired outcomes?
>   Is my talk part of a bigger event? If so, where do I fit in?
>   What is the format (other speakers, chairperson, etc)?
>   What is the theme of the whole event?
>   Will it be a straight talk or involve discussion?
>   Will there be questions?

Material:
>   What is the topic?
>   How much depth do you need?
>   What topics will others cover?
>   Do you want me to use visual aids?
>   How long have I got?

Venue:
>   Where is it?
>   How do I get there?
>   What is it like (purpose built lecture room, school hall, etc)?
>   What equipment does it have?

Objectives

Before you start to plan the presentation in detail you will need to be clear about your objectives. Questions to whoever has invited you will give you some broad aims and should give you guidance on the desired outcomes. Sometimes, however, this is not always clear and as the speaker you will have to define the objectives for yourself. Once you have defined aims and intended outcomes you should refine these into clear, audience centred objectives, then build your presentation to achieve these.

Preparing the presentation

Good preparation is the secret of a successful presentation! It will help you to:

- present the information the audience needs to know
- present in a way that is appropriate to your audience
- give you the confidence that you know what you are doing
- give a good account of your organization as well as yourself.

In addition, it will enable you to fit into the time allocated and present your material in a way that is logical, clear and relevant.

Stage 1

Research is the first stage in preparation. Gather together all the material you may need, even if you discard some later. You will also have found out the background to the event and how it is to be run, and collected information about the audience. Then, with these facts in mind, you will have set your objectives for the presentation.

Stage 2

Next you must decide on the presentation method to use. This could be a straight talk with no audience participation (an instructional talk); an opportunity to impart skills (vocational); or an opportunity for group interaction (discussion). Your decision will be based on the topic, size of audience, venue and time available.

Stage 3

From the material you have gathered and the method chosen, you will need to select and organize the content. You may discard some material, you may add more examples and anecdotes, but it should all be available by this stage.

You should note in the material the 'musts', 'shoulds' and 'coulds', ie, the essential information (*musts*), the useful information (*shoulds*) and information of interest but less important (the *coulds*).

Stage 4

When you have decided what you want to say, put it into a structure. Every presentation has three main parts:

- introduction (about 10% of the time)
- main body (about 75% of the time)
- conclusion (about 15% of the time).

Organize your material so that you know what is to go into each part.

The *introduction* will lay the foundation for your presentation and tell the audience what you are going to talk about. The *main body* is the main section where you present the information. The *conclusion* should recap on the main topics and round it off in a positive way.

Writing the brief

There are four main ways of writing up your notes for the presentation:

1. word for word as a script
2. write 'headlines' on a sheet of paper – these are the paragraph headings
3. write key points on cue cards as memory joggers
4. write structured notes that can be developed and modified as you talk.

Each of these methods has advantages and disadvantages and you need to select the one that will be best suited to your style, the situation and the topic. In time, as you become more confident in giving presentations, you are likely to be able to make your notes briefer.

Must, should and could

When you have written up your notes you will then need to go through and mark them up for *must*, *should* and *could*. This will enable you to be flexible if you have to alter the timing of your talk at the event.

Visual aids

If you are planning to use any visual aids you should mark your notes to remind yourself which you are using and when.

Timing the presentation

At the preparation stage you need to consider timing. You can do this by rehearsing the presentation and timing yourself. If you have to alter this timing at the last minute because the event is running late, or you have more time, you can use the 'musts, shoulds and coulds' to lengthen or shorten it very easily.

What if?

At the planning stage you should also consider what might go wrong. By considering all the potential problems, then planning solutions to them, you are less likely to get caught out and will be able to keep problems contained.

Visual aids

These can be used to enhance your talk, add clarity and interest. Poor visual aids will detract from what you say and may even confuse the audience. If you are going to use visual aids make sure they are well thought out and well prepared.

The main visual aids are:

- flip chart
- overhead projector
- 35mm slide projector
- video
- computer
- objects.

Each has advantages and disadvantages and you should select the most appropriate for the topic, audience and venue.

Handouts could also be useful to add detail or for later reference, especially where there are no power points for electrical equipment.

To use or not to use?

Before you decide to use a visual aid ask:

Does it assist understanding?
Does it help to emphasize a point?
Is it really necessary?
Does it provide additional information to what is being spoken?
Does it enhance or illustrate and not confuse?
Is it a good, clear, quality image?

Your answers to these questions should guide you in your decision.

Preparing good visuals

If you are to use visual aids they must be clear and well produced. For slides and overhead projector foils the points to remember in preparation are:

- keep to one format
- use a few lines and words on each slide
- ensure letter size is large enough to be read easily
- centre or range left text and headlines
- leave generous margins all round
- leave plenty of gaps and clear spaces
- simplify charts and diagrams for clarity.

Make sure you load your slides correctly or have your foils laid out in order to reach them easily. When using any visual aid make sure the screen is positioned so that the entire audience can see it clearly. Do not walk in front of the screen.

Don't let the technology take over – if it goes wrong be prepared to carry on without it!

Rehearsal and final preparation

Rehearsal

Rehearsal is a valuable tool to help even the most experienced presenter. Rehearsal can:

- help you to get timing right
- give you the comfort of knowing you are well prepared
- help you to write your brief in the most helpful way
- make sure you know when and how to use your visual aids most effectively.

There are a number of techniques for practising, which you can choose according to the help available and your preference. The main ones are practising alone in front of a mirror or recording yourself on a tape or cassette, or doing a trial run or in front of a friend or colleague.

Be careful to use language that the audience will understand, and avoid jargon. But try to use images and metaphor to keep it interesting and paint a picture for the audience.

Check out the venue and equipment

If possible visit the venue before your presentation to see what it is like. If you cannot go in advance make sure that you arrive in plenty of time to change things if you need to.

Check the venue for:

- location and travel arrangements
- loading and unloading facilities
- seating arrangements
- visibility, so that everyone can see you and your visual aids
- location of equipment and power supplies
- soundproofing and acoustics
- ventilation

and finally, get the feel of the place.

Check the equipment for:

- what is supplied (make, model etc)
- type of carousel or slides

- stand
- power supply
- screen
- spares (bulb, fuses)
- technical support
- operation (can you work it and is it working?)
- cue video if necessary.

Overcoming problems

There are a number of problems that may befall a presenter; being prepared will help to overcome these. Experienced presenters often carry a simple tool kit for minor problems, but you should always have an alternative to your visual aids in case all power or equipment fails.

Giving the presentation

First impressions

The impression you make when you stand up or walk onto the platform will set the tone for the whole presentation. Your body language says more about you than your words. Walk positively, look confident and the audience will believe in you. You need to get past the audience's emotional reaction to you before they will really hear what you are saying.

As well as positive body language, you must look smart and professional. This means dressing appropriately for your status, the occasion and the audience.

Body and voice

During the presentation your body language will continue to affect how the audience 'hears' you. Good eye contact is part of this, try to look at the audience and make eye contact with as many members as possible (but avoid your eyes darting around all over the place all the time!).

Consider what your bad habits are and work at eliminating these. Movement can be positive and help you to seem energetic, but fiddling with clothes and jewellery is irritating and distracting. If you are going to move around, make sure that you can work without your notes, or see them from where you stand.

The voice is the tool for communicating your words, so use it most effectively. If you have a quiet voice, work at projecting it better. If you have a high-pitched voice, work at lowering the pitch. Use pauses and changes of speed to keep your speech interesting.

Stress and nerves

Nervousness may be apparent in your voice; stress affects breathing and muscle tension, usually raising the pitch of your voice; your mouth dries, which makes it more difficult to talk. Stress will also deliver additional adrenaline which will make you talk faster.

Overcoming nerves and stress will help you to deliver a better presentation. Key points in overcoming nerves are:

- be prepared – knowing what you are doing is calming
- know the opening by heart – once you are under way it gets easier
- relax – before you begin, breathe deeply and move the parts of your upper body gently to loosen and relax
- have water nearby and take a small drink just before you start.

Anxieties can be overcome by:

- managing the material
- managing the resources
- managing the audience
- managing yourself.

Beginning

How you start will set the tone. Begin with a clear, positive statement that will interest the audience and make them take notice. Then when you have got their attention:

explain who you are and why you are here
give the objectives for your presentation
outline the topics

give a guide for the time it will take
explain how you want to handle questions (if at all)

and remember to keep the introduction brief but positive.

The main body

During the main part of your talk you need to impart information, but also work at keeping the attention of the audience. You can add variety with the content, break up the facts and figures with anecdotes and examples. Make it relevant to your listeners. Use your other media to add variety and use your voice to change the delivery – alter the pace and pitch and use pauses for effect.

Think about the words you are using, especially try to cut out the 'non-words' such as 'um', 'err' and 'you know'.

Dealing with questions and discussion

Questions and discussion can clarify and add interest, but you may need to handle some that are difficult. If you are well prepared you will be able to handle questions. If you do not know an answer, say so, but offer to find out.

Do not get into arguments or a long discussion with one individual; if you are assertive you can avoid this without being unpleasant. If other tactics fail, invoke the force of the rest of the audience.

Handling questions can be helped by:

anticipating questions and planning answers
controlling when you take questions
knowing your topic well and being prepared
listening carefully to the question – make notes if you
    want
'translate' or paraphrase unclear questions
restate questions to the audience in case all did not hear it
learn the techniques for dealing with difficult questions
avoid long discussions only of interest to one questioner
keep eye contact with the questioner, break it when
    enlisting the help of the group
give positive responses; where the answer has to be
    negative try to end on a positive note

remember that questions give you an opportunity to add credibility to your presentation.

The finale

Use the last part of the presentation to draw the event to a good conclusion. Recap on the main points of what you have said and make any recommendations you wish on your key points.

Finish on a decisive note and thank the audience for listening. Do not include any new ideas, but be upbeat and positive.